Ancient and Modern Methods of

Growing Extraordinary Marijuana

**Ancient and Modern Methods of
Growing Extraordinary Marijuana**
ISBN: 978-0-914171-94-2
ISBN: 0-914171-94-1
Copyright 1975 by Kistone Press
Copyright 1998 by Twentieth Century Alchemist and
Ronin Publishng, Inc. (Revised edition)

Published and Distributed by
RONIN PUBLISHING, INC.
P.O. Box 22900
Oakland, CA 94609
roninpub.com

Project Editor: Sebastian Orfali
Editors: Adam Gottlieb, Dan Joy
Cover Design: Judy July
Illustrations: Larry Todd, Robert Connell Clarke

Distributed by Perseus
Printed in the United States of America

Ancient and Modern Methods of

Growing Extraordinary
Marijuana

by Adam Gottlieb

Ronin Publishing, Inc.
Berkeley, CA
roninpub.com

Notice to Reader

Table of Contents

Introduction

About Marijuana

 Marijuana is a weed. There is nothing more to making it grow than putting the seed in the right place at the right time. In the hills of central Mexico, many farmers simply scatter the seed upon the field in springtime and forget about the plants until harvest time. And what they harvest is dynamite grass because the soil and climate are optimal for producing high potency hemp. On the other hand, there are roadsides in the USA where marijuana flourishes for miles. But even the uptight local authorities are not much concerned about it, since it takes three joints the size of cigars to produce even the mildest buzz.

The difference between Mexican hill grass and the American roadside hemp is due mainly to the amounts of active THC (tetrahydrocannabinol) present. Primo Mexican grass may contain 3-5% THC, while Midwestern roadside may contain only 1/4-1%. This is not to say that Mexican grass is good, while US grass is garbage. It is simply that the environmental conditions in most of Mexico are inclined to produce higher quality marijuana than are the conditions in much of the USA.

Another factor that influences both the potency and the quality of the high involves the balance of different cannabinoid materials in the plant. Marijuana resin contains several isomers of THC. The delta-1 isomer is the most prevalent and most potent. Some of this THC may be present in the form of THC acid. THC acid is not active, but much of it is converted

Mexican *Cannabis* (Michoacan variety)
Drawing by Robert Connell Clarke
reprinted from *Marijuana Botany*.

to THC if the tops are properly dried after harvesting. Grass grown in hot, dry climates with a long growing season tends to contain more THC and less THC acid than the North American crops.

Northern grass also contains a greater percentage of cannabidiol than that from hotter climates. Ganja and hashish resin from the hot, dry countries contain only minimal amounts of cannabidiol while northern grass may contain as much as 33% cannabidiol in the oil extract. Although cannabidiol produces no high, it does act as an inducer and prolonger of sleep. This is especially true when it is taken with other active cannabinoids. It is because of the differences in cannabidiol content that some types of grass are stimulating while others produce grogginess.

It is also believed that ultraviolet light—which is more intense in the highlands of the more southerly climates—may convert many of the less active isomers and cannabinoids to more potent forms. Laboratory experiments were conducted at the University of Illinois in which pure cannabidiol was exposed to UV light resulting in a 2% conversion to active THC.

It has been further noted that polyploid varieties of marijuana—which have developed either through environmental conditions or through treatment with colchicine—tend to contain a higher percentage of THC and a lower percentage of cannabidiol and less desirable cannabinoids than normal diploids contain.

Part One of this book covers the fundamentals of growing quality marijuana. Part Two reviews methods used to produce marijuana of extraordinary quality, highlighting the time-tested agricultural traditions of India and Mexico. Part Three describes contributions to marijuana potency from high-tech horticulture. *Growing Extraordinary Marijuana* concludes with a brief look at the importance of quality in marijuana cultivation in light of the plant's increasingly recognized medicinal value.

Part I

Basic Cultivation

1. Starting The Plants

 Many cultivators in the USA go to great extremes to prepare the seed for planting. They soak the seeds overnight in water or wrap them in wet newspapers and incubate them in an oven for 8 hours. All this is unnecessary. Pre-sprouting does nothing to increase the percentage of germination, hasten maturity, or improve either the quantity or quality of the grass. All it does is speed up the germination period by a few days. Marijuana seeds may be either started in a seed-box or nursery and later transplanted to their final location, or started in their ultimate location.

Viability of Seeds

Much has been written on how to tell if seeds are viable or not. Most methods are of value only to people who have excess time to squander. In almost any lid of grass, 80% of the seeds are viable. Colombian grass, or grass that has been buried, often has a larger percentage of dead seeds. These are usually hollow and collapse when pressed between the thumb and index finger. It is best simply to plant all seeds. What comes up comes up.

Selecting Seeds

The choice of seed can make a difference in results. Seeds from superior breeds of grass are inclined to produce superior plants, at least for the first generation or two. This is why growers often save the seeds for planting when they run across great weed.

Seeds

Germinating Seeds

When growers use a seed box for germinating marijuana, they use one in which the soil is at least 4 inches deep. The soil is kept moist but not soggy. If the soil is too wet, the seeds may rot. If the seed bed is outside and the nights are cold, it is covered at night with tarpaulin or glass. The seedlings should sprout within a week. Sometimes it may take up to 3 weeks.

Seedlings

The seedlings need full exposure to sunlight for the whole day or the equivalent in artificial light. If the seedlings are over-watered they may develop stem rot and die. It is best that the soil on the surface is dry, while that 1/2 inch beneath contains moisture. Growers accomplish this by watering from the bottom rather than the top by placing the flower pot or seed bed in a pan of water until just enough moisture has been taken up. The soil is never allowed to dry out more than an inch below the surface.

If the young plants are started in the field, growers sprinkle or water via irrigation trenches. The morning hours are the best for watering whether the plants are grown indoors or outdoors. Seeds are not sown outdoors until the rainy season has passed unless the seedlings can be protected from the excess water.

When the plants are 2-4 weeks old and 6-8 inches tall, they are thinned out if they are growing in their ultimate location, or transplanted if they have been started elsewhere. The weaker plants are removed. The healthier plants which are retained are spaced 2-3 feet apart in rows 3-4 feet apart. Rows run north and south so that plants get maximum exposure to the sun. Growers take care not to damage the roots when transplanting or thinning.

2. Transplanting

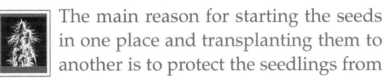 The main reason for starting the seeds in one place and transplanting them to another is to protect the seedlings from wind, late frost, or the attack of birds. Any plant permitted to grow in the same place it was started avoids the shock of transplanting and is likely to be healthier and more productive.

Late afternoon is the best time for transplanting because freshly thinned or transplanted plants will wilt if they are exposed to the hot sun. On the morning of the day that transplanting will take place, growers generously water both their plants and the field into which they are to be transplanted. Transplanting can be done in the earlier part of the day if the sky is overcast. In this case, watering of the plants and field can be performed about two hours before transplanting.

At this point, growers usually treat the soil with one of the widely available commercial formulas for reducing transplant shock and helping plants recover more quickly. Growers make sure that there is plenty of soil kept about the roots when they lift young plants from the ground. If the plants are grown in flower pots, one pot 10 inches in diameter is used for each plant. Fertilizer is not used on the plants for at least two weeks after transplanting or thinning.

Testing for pH Levels

Seedlings fare best when the soil into which they are transplanted is similar to that in which they were germinated. The ideal soil for growing marijuana is a light sandy loam—high in nitrogen and potassium—with good drainage and an acid/alkaline balance between pH 6.5 and pH 7.5. Soil test kits are available at most garden shops or at Sears. Acidity can be increased by the judicious addition of aluminum sulfate. Alkalinity is increased by adding hydrated lime.

Growers test and adjust pH of the soil every month because some tap water contains residues which increase the acidity of the soil.

3. Artifical Lighting Systems

 Marijuana cultivated outdoors needs full sunlight to grow profusely, mature properly, and produce a high resin content. If grown indoors under artificial illumination, plants need to receive about the same light period as they would receive naturally out of doors. Various kinds of artificial light are used by indoor growers. Each type of light has its own advantages and disadvantages.

Growers control the periods of light and darkness so that they fall at the same time each day, but it does not matter whether they coincide with the actual times of day and night outside.

Fluorescent Lights

Fluorescent lights, which generate light by passing electricity through gaseous vapor kept at low pressure, were once the form of artificial light most commonly used for growing marijuana indoors.

Some fluorescent lamps come close to duplicating the spectrum of sunlight, but they simply are not powerful enough for efficient growing of marijuana. Fluorescent lights are still, however, very good for rooting cuttings, as the kind of light they emit promotes root growth.

High Intensity Discharge Lamps

High Intensity Discharge (HID) lamps generate light by running electric current through highly pressurized gas. HID lamps, which include metal halide and high pressure sodium vapor lamps, are now preferred because they can be used to create the same patterns of growth by which marijuana responds to natural sunlight.

Metal Halide Lamps

Clear metal halide HID lamps are now the artificial light source most widely used by people who grow marijuana indoors. Metal halide HIDs are the most efficient and brightest artificial source of white light presently available for growing. Clear metal halides are good for growing seedlings, for bringing the seedlings to adulthood, and for promoting the growth of flowering tops.

Sodium Vapor Lamps

High pressure sodium vapor lamps produce even more light than metal halides, but the light they emit is biased towards the yellow-orange-red end of the spectrum. This is why they generate an orange glow of a color comparable to that of the harvest sun. This kind of light is particularly good for promoting flower production. Some growers add high pressure sodium vapor lamps to their lighting system during flowering, increasing the volume and weight of their flower yield by 20% or even more.

Placing Lights

Lights are kept six to twelve inches above the tops of the plants, or two to three feet above if the plants are very young, tender seedlings. If the lights are attached to a sheet of plywood which is suspended above the plants by chains or ropes on pulleys, they can be raised as the plants grow. The surface of the plywood behind the lamps—as well as the walls and floor of the growing chamber—are either covered with aluminum foil or painted white in order to reflect and make available as much illumination as possible.

Using Timers

Growers usually connect timers to the lights so that they will go on and off at the proper times. Lights cannot be left on continuously or for longer than 14 hours a day because to do so would prevent the plants from maturing and flowering.

Indoor Marijuana Horticulture by Jorge Cervantes offers a wealth of information on different kinds of lights and how they can be used for indoor marijuana cultivation.

4. Using Lights To Maximize Flowering

 Growers set up their systems to ensure that the plants are subject to twelve hours of absolutely uninterrupted darkness during each twenty-four hour period to bring on flowering. An even twelve hours per day of light *versus* darkness makes plants between two and twelve months old start to flower within one to three weeks. The younger the plant, the longer it takes to begin flowering. Less than twelve hours of light won't bring on flowering any quicker, and may actually decrease the size of the flower harvest, whereas giving the plants more than twelve hours of light delays the onset of flowering.

The flowering period can be made to last up to several weeks longer by gradually reducing the daily period of light received by the plants from thirteen or fourteen hours down to twelve hours, as the corresponding period of darkness slowly increases to twelve hours. Growers use this technique to simulate the natural change of season, an effect which can be enhanced by exposing the plants to intense light from the red end of the spectrum to stimulate flower production. They accomplish this by the addition of high pressure sodium vapor lamps.

5. Pruning & Harvesting

When the plants are 12 inches tall, they are ready for pruning. Lower leaf-branches that are losing their vigorous appearance are broken off. The tops are clipped back.

Increasing Foliage

Pruning causes the plant to branch out and become more abundant in foliage. Clipping can be repeated from time to time until the flower stalks begin to appear.

Clipping causes the plant to branch out.

Harvesting

When the female flower tops have begun to turn brownish or yellowish, they are ready to be harvested. They can be clipped off and dried in the sun or indoors at room temperature.

Drying And THC

Drying is sometimes done in an oven, but this practice has a negative effect on the potency of the end product. When the leaves and tops are fresh, most of the THC is present in the form of tetrahydrocannabinolic acid, which must be converted to THC to have any effect. Slow drying causes much of the THC acid to change into to THC, but oven drying can be too rapid for this conversion to take place.

6. Basics of Breeding

When growers set out to breed marijuana, it's important that they know what they want to achieve. They must know what desirable qualities they want to breed into a strain that it lacks, as well as what undesirable qualities the strain has that they want to breed out. A grower might want to breed in the tendency to produce flowering tops of high potency, for example, while breeding out a tendency for the plants to be too small.

Selecting Parents

Once growers have established clear goals for breeding, they select the parent strains to be used. They select in favor of the characteristics they desire, and against those characteristics that are undesirable. In order to make an intelligent selection of parent strains, the growers have to know which characteristics of marijuana can be altered through breeding.

Cross-Fertilization

Hybridization is the process of the mixing gene pools. Hybridization takes place randomly in nature, but cultivators perform controlled, directed hybridization called *cross-pollination, cross-fertilization,* or *crossing*. A simple way to cross-fertilize is to plant two strains side-by-side to produce seeds that grow into hybrid offspring which will have some of the characteristics of each of the parent strains. Growers select the offspring with the most favorable characteristics for further breeding.

Advantages Of Hybrids

Vigorous, healthy plants from genetically diverse strains—for instance, strains taken from two distant parts of the world—are most likely to produce sizable, hardy offspring due to a genetic phenomenon known as *hybrid vigor,* in which favorable characteristics carried by the dominant genes mask the unfavorable features carried by the recessive genes of the other strain.

Part II

Ancient Secrets

Hindu-Kush *Cannabis indica*
Drawing by Robert Connell Clarke reprinted from
Marijuana Botany.

7. Cultivation
In Mexico And India

Beyond the fundamentals of cultivating and harvesting decent marijuana, growers use many techniques to increase the potency of their plants, some of which have been practiced for generations in India and Mexico. Farmers in many regions of the Indian subcontinent and the highlands of the Mexican state of Oaxaca have long been known for producing extraordinary marijuana. They have a wealth of secrets to share.

Mexican Volcanic Highlands

Some of the finest Mexican marijuana is cultivated in the volcanic highlands of the state of Oaxaca in southern Mexico. Here the mineral-rich soil, the hot, dry climate, and the prevalence of ultraviolet light work together to produce grass of great potency and stimulating quality.

Ganja Farmers of India

For many thousands of years, farmers of India have cultivated some of the strongest marijuana in the world. The most potent form is known as *ganja* and consists of the dried flowering tops of the female plant, which have become coated with resin as a result of not being allowed to set seed freely.

Although much of the superiority of the plants grown in India may be credited to the local climate and the probability that the strain of seed used is the consequence of ages of careful breeding (most likely *Cannabis indica* rather than *Cannabis sativa*), there can be no doubt that many of the cultivation techniques employed by these farmers greatly enhance both the quantity and quality of the active resin.

It will be obvious that a few of the Indian practices discussed—like that of growing the plant in the mouth of a dead cobra—are either of dubious efficacy or are not feasible for growers in the modern West. These are mentioned to give the reader a taste of the colorful and arcane nature of the ancient marijuana growing traditions in this part of the world. The rest of the Indian techniques described, however, have proven their value and have been handed down from father to son for thousands of years.

8. Selecting And Preparing Soil

 It is universally agreed that marijuana requires a light, well drained soil that has not been exhausted by previous crops. In the Indian state of Bengal a field is selected which has lain fallow for the previous two years or which has supported only light crops such as mustard or pulses during that time. The field, of course, is open to the sun and not shadowed by trees or nearby hilltops.

In the Central Provinces of India such as Khandwa, the preferred soils are *pandhar*—a white soil mixed with ashes and sweepings from the village, and *mand*—a light yellow *alluvium*, a kind of sand or clay deposited by a body of water and permeable by moisture. Black clayish soil or *regur* is used when cannabis is raised for hemp, but it is not favorable for producing plants of high potency.

Readying The Field

In Bengal the field is first ploughed and then liberally dressed with surface soil from the surrounding areas. After about a week, this soil dries out and is treated with cow manure and reploughed. This is followed by breaking up the soil with an instrument called a harrow. The ploughing and harrowing are repeated periodically until planting time. It is believed that the more the ploughing, the better the crop.

In Khandwa, unlike Bengal and most other states of India, the same field is used year after year. Heavy manuring is not employed. Instead, a mixture of household refuse, cow dung, and ashes is ploughed in at the rate of 16 to 20 cart loads per acre. In the region of India known as Berar white land is preferred. Black soil contains too much clay, is too stiff, and has to be made lighter with heavy manuring.

9. Planting For High Potency

 In the Indian state of Bengal a plot of land is selected near the homestead as a nursery for starting the seedlings. The plot chosen consists of high, light sandy loam. To be sure of its dryness, the farmer usually selects an open area where a tuberous-rooted grass-like vegetable called *matha (Cyperus rotundus L.)* grows. The land is not manured, but is ploughed three times before planting. Planting in rainy weather is avoided because wet ground rots the seeds.

When the seedlings are 4 or 5 weeks old and from 6 to 12 inches high, they are transplanted to the field. First, the field is ploughed, harrowed, made into ridges, smoothed, and beaten down with the hand. The smaller plants are planted in higher, drier fields where they send down their roots quickly and easily and then grow up more swiftly.

A month after transplanting, the field is carefully weeded. Two weeks later, the ridges are hoed down as far as possible without injuring the roots and are well fertilized with oil cake, the solid residue left after pressing oil from seeds such as olive or sesame, or a mixture of manure and oil cake. Then the ridges are rebuilt over the fertilizer.

In the Himalayan area of India the seeds are often sown directly in the field. Chaff is then scattered over the field to protect the seed from the birds. In the Indian Punjab the seed is soaked overnight in cow's milk and water before being sown broadcast in the fields.

Cultivation practices of the Kistna district of India are essentially similar to those of Bengal. The crop usually follows millet, dry rice, coriander, tobacco, indigo or chilies, but sometimes hemp is grown in successive years. The nursery is made on the dam of a water tank and measures 6 x 60 feet. The soil is dug with a crowbar, finely tilled, and leveled. Seed is scattered upon the ground and covered by hand with soil. The bed is hand-watered as needed for the next two months. When the plants are two feet high, the tops are removed and within a week they put out numerous side-branches. They are then transplanted to the field.

10. Fertilizing Ganja

Although the fertilizers most commonly used in India are cow dung, sheep dung, ashes, and household refuse, there are several unique fertilizers which many ganja farmers swear by for cultivating the highest potency product.

On the Punjab plains serpent excreta and swallow dung are often used. In the Madras states the decomposed bodies of dead snakes are believed to be the finest fertilizer for potent ganja. Some farmers believe that there is a special advantage to placing the seeds in the mouths of freshly killed serpents and planting the whole thing. Farmers of Sind sometimes bury a dead snake beneath each plant or water the plants with Jimson Weed infusion or water from a hooka pipe through which ganja or charas has been smoked.

Similar practices may be found in the Kistna district. Here decomposed serpent bodies and the dung of pigeons or other fowl are considered the best ganja fertilizers. Sometimes the seed or seedling is planted in the mouth of a dead dog or serpent which has been buried in a suitable position. Often, water soiled from washing fish is poured on the ground around the plant. It is no surprise to anyone who has used commercial fish emulsion fertilizer on their plants that such experienced cultivators have found fish washings to be an efficacious plant food.

One of the strangest methods for increasing the potency of marijuana plants employed in Sind involves attempting to poison the plant by the bite of a cobra. When particularly strong ganja is required, the cultivators of Bhopawar water each plant with opium dissolved in water. They also believe that transplanting the young plant into the mouth of a dead venomous snake—cobras are preferred—renders greater strength to the ganja.

11. Directing Growth

 In Bengal the lower branches of the plant are removed 2 or 3 months after transplanting to the field. This helps to give the plant a pyramidal shape that brings the flowering tops as close together as possible and prevents the formation of ganja too close to the ground, where it would get mud-caked. Immediately after pruning, there is another ploughing and harrowing between the ridges. Then another application of fertilizer is given, after which the ridges are rebuilt.

In Nepal when the plants put forth fine down, the tips are cut off and the larger leaves are plucked. The plant is also shaken from time to time so that the down may fall off. This causes a large number of branches and fine leaves to be produced. These fine leaves get twisted and stuck together and are called *latta*.

Another pruning method used in most parts of India involves roughly twisting the stem at the base of the plant which stunts the plant's growth and causes it to produce more ganja. In some areas the flower heads are similarly twisted to prevent overbranching.

Horizontal Growth Techniques

In the Indian region of Mysore one month old seedlings are transplanted into pits—each one 1 foot deep, dug at intervals of 3 feet—and well manured. The young plants are watered daily for a month or so. Then the stem of each plant is twisted just above the ground, and the plant itself is bent horizontally to the level of the earth to prevent vertical growth and induce the development of side-branches.

Outdoor growers in the United States and other areas use a somewhat similar method of training plants to grow horizontally in order to increase flower yield. This method, a kinder, gentler—and easier—version of the traditional Mysore technique, is one of the least traumatic ways to get a plant to increase massively its production of flower tops. This form of horizontal training does not start until the plants have already started to develop substantial flowering clusters at the top of the main stem, which doesn't usually occur until the plants are at least four feet tall.

Plants are bent horizontally to induce side-branching.

Training The Plant

A string is attached to a point about two-thirds of the way up the main stem and a stake is driven into the soil three or four feet away from the plant's base. The string is used to pull the plant over in a gentle curve, bending it as far over as possible without overly stressing it. Then the string is tied to the stake in such a way as to maintain this position. This procedure usually results in the very top of the plant being pulled about one and a half feet away from its original position.

After the plant is given a few days to adapt to this new posture, the length of the string binding the plant to the stake is decreased by six to twelve inches, thus gently pulling the plant into a slightly more horizontal position. This operation is repeated every few days until the top third of the plant is truly horizontal.

As the plant is getting trained towards horizontal growth, its higher branches will start to grow vertically and then begin to put out horizontal branches of their own. As result, flowering clusters begin to develop profusely. The yield of flower tops is likely to be exponentially greater than that which would have been produced by the plant had it not been subjected to this procedure. More details on training plants for horizontal growth can be found in *The Cultivator's Handbook of Marijuana* by Bill Drake.

12. Stressing The Plant

 It is now well known that cannabis resins are produced as a protective coating against the hot sun and are inclined
to be more abundant in hot, dry, climates.

The marijuana farmers of Oaxaca, Mexico
subject their plants to several operatons which
influence their chemistry and increase resin production. The philosophy of these farmers is
that a normal, healthy plant which has grown
under comfortable conditions does not produce
the best product for human use. To develop a
potent product, the plant must be tortured by
environmental extremes, unusual pruning
methods, and the techniques of crucifixion.
This philosophy is probably rooted in the Chris-
tian-Pagan concept of spiritual ripening and
salvation through suffering.

The ganja farmers of India have some similar techniques for stressing their plants to in-

crease potency. These Indian methods, however, do not appear to be rooted in any underlying philosophy similar to that of the Mexicans, but probably emerge instead from thousands of years of observing that plants that have been damaged or challenged in specific ways yielded a product of extraordinary quality.

Removing Tips

In Mexico, when the plant is just beyond its seedling stage, the tip or *apical meristem* is clipped. The tip is where a hormone called *auxin* that promotes longitudinal growth is produced. Other important hormones are produced here as well. The removal of the source of these hormones causes the formation of side shoots (or *lateral meristems*). The clipping or pinching off of the new tips is repeated once a week and causes the plant to take on a bushy, urn-like shape. Shoots which would normally fill the interior of the bush are also clipped. In its mature state a plant so treated will develop a thick, crystalline coating of resin.

Constant clipping also affects leaf production. It causes less of the large, broad, palmate leaves to occur and results in a predominance of ball-like clusters of smaller, finer leaves in which the resins are more highly concentrated. These are similar to *latta* produced by the ganja farmers of Nepal.

Wedging

The Indian stem-twisting practice described earlier often causes a vertical split to occur near the base of the plant. Occasionally, the grower will wedge some foreign material into the split. This is supposed to increase the production of resin in the plant. Growers often deliberately split the stem with a knife.

One of the most unusual methods of controlling growth is carried out in Burma. About a month before maturity, when the stem of the plant is about the thickness of a finger, the stem is split and a piece of wood is inserted. A basket—or sometimes a light earthen chatty— with a mouth about a foot in diameter is placed over the flower-bearing branches which are gathered together, thrust into the vessel, and kept there for about a month. This prevents further growth of the plant and makes the flower heads grow thick.

In the Indian region of Orissa, the stem is punctured or cut, and a piece of broken tile is inserted in the opening. In Gangpur, cross-incisions are made in the stem, and a piece of opium or some other intoxicant is inserted. In the Kistna district the stem is split, and opium or arsenic is tightly bound in the cleft. The use of opium in the split to improve the narcotic quality of the ganja is also practiced in Sind, Berar, and Nepal. The Nepalese farmers also sometimes use a piece of clove or bhirosa wood in place of the opium. In some areas asafetida gum is used instead of opium for this purpose.

A piece of wood, tile, or other foregin material is wedged into the split at the base of the stem.

These practices have their parallels in the USA, where some growers now insert a thumbtack in the lower stem to stimulate resin reproduction, and in Mexico where the technique of "crucifixion" is used.

Crucifixion

Constant pinching to remove tips as sometimes practiced in Mexico alters the pigmentation of the plant. The changes wrought upon auxin production cause an accumulation of *cyanins*, pigments that lend a reddish color to the plant. The variety of marijuana widely known as "Panama red" is the result of such treatment.

When the blood-like color appears, the plants are crucified. This procedure is similar to the wedging technique practiced by the ganja farmers of India and the insertion of thumbtacks in the stem base now in vogue among many northern cultivators. In Oaxaca, instead of making one insertion in the base of the stem, two splinters of wood, such as toothpicks, are inserted at right angles to each other, forming a cross when viewed from above. This causes an increase in the formation of active resins in the flower tops.

13. Removing Males

A practice common among the ganja farmers of India is the removal or destruction of male plants prior to flowering. This is done for several reasons: male plants are not as potent as females and do not produce the resin that is necessary for ganja; the male plant is believed also to produce a more giddy and less desirable high than the female; and removal of the male plants gives the female more room to grow.

The main reason for extirpating the males, sometimes called emasculation, is that once the female has been pollinated by the male, she will cease to produce resins and her potency will rapidly diminish. If a farmer in India is asked why remove the males, he is likely to answer: "What would happen if a ram were let loose among a flock of ewes?"

Benefits Of Seedlessness

The preferred form of ganja in India is that which contains little or no seeds. Such a product is similar in appearance to sinsemilla marijuana grown occasionally in Mexico, but more resinous and potent than the New World product. The seedless product is more potent than that which has been pollinated. Tops devoid of seed are a great convenience when preparing them for a smoke, especially when the high content of sticky resin may cause the seeds to adhere to the ganja.

Identifying Sex

In some parts of India a professional extirpator known as a *poddar* is hired to inspect the young plants and remove those which he recognizes as male. It is said to be a very difficult task to make a distinction at this stage of growth. Most other cultivators in both the East and West find that there is no way to tell male from female plants until they have begun to send forth flower stalks.

Most farmers are satisfied to wait until these stalks appear before attempting to cull out the males. Even when the *poddar's* services are used, he must inspect the field once more when the flower stalks first show to make certain that no males remain and to remove any hermaphrodites—mutant females bearing male blossoms. Actually there is no need to remove the males until shortly before the first flowers open.

14. Harvesting Ganja And Bhang

 The ganja of India is always harvested on a dry, sunny day. Harvesting is never conducted on a rainy, damp, or even cloudy day when rain might occur. Much of the quality of Central Asian ganja is due to the dryness of the climate during the growing season. Cultivators of all provinces agree that after the plant has begun to flower in clusters and the resinous matter has formed, rain spoils the ganja. The usual indication that the ganja is ready to harvest is that the leaves and flower-heads turn yellowish to brownish and the larger leaves begin to fall.

Using Male Plants

Much mention has been made of the psychoactive superiority of the female plant and the weeding out of the males. This is not to say that the male plant is entirely useless. In

India the carefully cultivated flower tops of the female are taken for ganja or charas, both of which are usually smoked, whereas the leaves of the male plants, along with the lower leaves of the female, are harvested as *bhang*.

Bhang is sometimes smoked by the very poor, but more often it is made into an intoxicating confection or beverage. Recipes made from bhang—or regular quality grass—can be found in *The Art and Science of Cooking with Cannabis* by Adam Gottlieb.

15. Forcing A Second Flowering

 In Mexico some farmers bend each flower stalk sharply at its base so that circulation is cut off at the top. The flower heads are allowed to dry on the plant for a week and then collected. Then the plants will usually put forth a second crop of flowers after the first harvest.

When this happens, some cultivators will uproot the whole plant and hang it upside down for a week or so. This is said to prevent any THC in the tops from being drawn back by gravity towards the base of the plant and to cause some of the THC in the body of the plant to go to the tops. Only sunny days are appropriate for harvesting. Mature flower tops can be ruined by exposure to rain or drizzle.

Many indoor growers use a technique related to that of the Mexican outdoor growers for bringing about a second flower harvest. In fact, Bill Drake, author of *The Cultivator's Hand-book of Marijuana*, holds that such operations are more effective if performed indoors under lights.

Plants Are Cut Back

First, the plants are cut back to about three feet in height, yielding the first harvest. Then about three-quarters of the remaining leaf clusters are pinched off, without clipping any branches, leaving only the healthiest leaf clusters.

Intense Lighting

The plants are then watered and fertilized well. The cycle of twelve hours each of light and darkness for accelerating flowering is maintained, and the lights are lowered to as short a distance as possible above the tops of the plants. Powerful side-lighting is often also used.

The Second Crop

A new crop of flower buds will start to appear within two weeks, and within six to eight weeks a second harvest of sinsemilla flowers, equivalent to about 1/3 to 2/3 the weight of the original harvest, will be produced. With very healthy plants indoors under lights, it is often possible to perform the entire operation again for a third harvest.

Additional details of flower forcing technique can be found in *The Cultivator's Handbook of Marijuana* by Bill Drake. *Marijuana Flower Forcing: Secrets of Designer Growing* by Tom Flowers is a concise and accessible work devoted entirely to this subject.

Part III

Modern Methods

16. New Cultivation Discoveries

 It is unfortunate that when a substance becomes illegal or taboo, scientific research on the material usually comes to a near halt. Such has been the case with marijuana. Still, despite the present biochemical dark ages, some knowledge of the plant's nature has been acquired.

Most notable is the work of Sister Mary Louis Tibeau of the University of Wisconsin. Her discoveries regarding the influence of soil chemistry upon the plant's growth and resin production has been of great value to serious cultivators. The attempt of researchers Warmke and Davidson during World War II to improve the quality of hemp fiber in the male by grafting it to hops root stocks failed, but led to the discovery that a hops plant grafted to a marijuana root stock will contain cannabis resins.

Experiments conducted by individual growers have disclosed many other important facets about the nature of cannabis and what is best for its development and potency. There also have been several recent discoveries which apply to the improvement of any plant. Some of the techniques which are most likely to improve the quantity and quality of the marijuana harvest will now be examined.

17. Mineral Nutrition

 The amounts of certain minerals in the soil affect the growth and chemistry of the marijuana plant at different stages of life. Abundant nitrogen during early development promotes growth and leaf production. Deprivation of nitrogen—after most growth has been attained, but before flowering—stimulates the production of resins.

Similarly, plenty of potassium in early life will promote profuse foliage and growth, while too much in later life will inhibit resin production. Too much calcium during the plant's first stages will stunt growth and during later life will inhibit resin. Yet the plant has need for much calcium during middle life. Adequate magnesium during early and middle life helps to make plants tall, and an increase of this material later on stimulates rapid maturity and resin production.

The Ideal

The ideal pattern of mineral distribution would be: high nitrogen and potassium, adequate magnesium, and low calcium during the plant's first 6-8 weeks; sustained abundance of nitrogen, potassium, and magnesium and increased calcium during the second 6-8 weeks; and sharply decreased nitrogen, potassium, and calcium and increased magnesium after the 12th or 16th week.

The issue confronted by growers is how to control the soil chemistry in accordance with this pattern of nutrition. It is easy enough to increase the calcium and magnesium at the appropriate times. But it is almost impossible to decrease the nitrogen, potassium, and calcium contents during later life.

When marijuana is grown in soil, this might be accomplished either by estimating the amount of these elements which will be depleted by the appropriate time or by transplanting to different soils for each life period.

The first method requires continuous soil testing and accurate calculations. The second method threatens the plant with transplant shock.

Hydroponics Is Best

The best way to control soil chemistry is to employ a neutral growing medium such as clean sand or vermiculite, watered with a properly balanced mineral solution which can be replaced with a different solution at the proper times. In other words, the best way to control mineral balance is through hydroponics

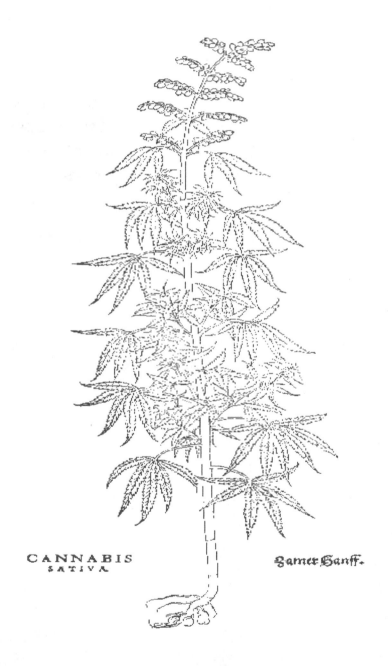

CANNABIS
SATIVA

Zamer Hanff.

18. Hydroponics
For Nutrition Control

 Hydroponics can be conducted outdoors, in a greenhouse, or indoors under artificial light. It can be done in
individual growing cans, or in a growing tank.

Hydroponic Hardware

Out of doors, growers use a sealed wood
or concrete pool about 18 inches deep. The
table or pool is usually constructed of 1/2 inch
thick exterior plywood and sealed with concrete, epoxy, tar, or any other suitable water-
proofing material. Zinc or galvanized metal
are not used unless they are coated to prevent
toxic contact with the solution and plants. Circulation is necessary to maintain aeration and
to keep the mineral salts evenly distributed.

If a can or a very small table is used, the solution is drained and poured back into the container. The general construction of hydroponic containers is shown in the illustration. Details of design, as well as complete set-up and maintenance procedures for a more sophisticated hydroponics system are described in *Marijuana Hydroponics: High-Tech Water Culture* by Daniel Storm.

Hydroponic Containers

Hydroponic Growing Media

Sometimes crushed rock, gravel, cinders, granite fragments, or brick chips are used as hydroponic media. The minerals present in these materials may upset the balance of nutrients, so many hydroponic marijuana cultivators choose instead to use clean, coarse builder's sand or beach sand that has been washed thoroughly to remove salts and organic residues. Perlite and vermiculite are commercially available hydroponic growing media that are also often used by hydroponic marijuana growers.

Rockwool

A unique soilless growing medium called *rockwool* is on the cutting edge in hydroponic marijuana cultivation. First developed for use as a form of insulation, rockwool has become a commonplace feature of commercial European greenhouse vegetable gardens. Rockwool is made from molten stone spun into fine fibers which solidify and are then granulated or pressed into sheets, blocks or cubes. Rockwool is cheaper than soil and holds far more water. It is completely sterile, easily adapted to different containers, and provides excellent aeration. Rockwool also makes it very easy to control the quantities of nutrients that the plants absorb, although pH levels are closely monitored and adjusted when rockwool is used for growing marijuana.

Jorge Cervantes' appendix to *Marijuana Hydroponics: High-Tech Water Culture* by Daniel Storm features further information on rockwool and its use, as well as suggestions as to where agricultural rockwool—as opposed to insulation rockwool, which is treated with a substance toxic to plants—can be obtained.

19. Hydroponic Nutrient Solutions

 A three-stage formula for growing solutions is used by sophisticated hydroponic marijuana cultivators for maintaining mineral balance.

Distilled or de-ionized water is used to prepare all solutions. Tap water is never used. Also included in this chapter is the formula for trace mineral solution (TMS). This contains minerals which are required in small amounts throughout the plant's life. TMS is an ingredient in each of the three growing solutions described on the next page.

Seeds are germinated in the growing medium with plain water which is replaced with solution #1 after two weeks.

SOLUTION #1:

Ammonium nitrate 9 g, calcium nitrate 1.2 g, magnesium sulfate 1.2 g, potassium chloride 1.6 g, potassium hydrophosphate 1.2 g, potassium nitrate 1.2 g, potassium sulfate 2.8 g, TMS 1/4 oz, water 1 gallon. This solution is used after the second week for 6-8 weeks.

SOLUTION #2:

Calcium nitrate 2.5 g, magnesium sulfate 1.2 g, potassium chloride 1.5 g, potassium hydrophosphate 1.2 g, potassium sulfate 2.8 g, TMS 1/4 oz, water 1 gallon. This solution is used after 6-8 weeks for the next 6-8 weeks.

SOLUTION #3:

Calcium nitrate 500 mg, magnesium chloride 2 g, magnesium sulfate 2 g, potassium hydrophosphate 3 g, TMS 1/4 oz, water 1 gallon. This solution is used during the remainder of the plant's life.

TRACE MINERAL SOLUTION (TMS):

Boric acid 750 mg, copper sulfate 500 mg, ferric citrate 7 g, magnesium sulfate 1 g, sodium molybdate 500 mg, zinc sulfate 500 mg, water 1 quart.

Before a new solution is introduced, the table or growing container is drained of the previous liquids, and the growing medium is rinsed with fresh water. These drainings and rinsings still contain much valuable mineral salts and growers usually recycle them into a garden or pour them into a compost heap.

20. Buriable Soaker Pipe

In recent decades the use of *buriable soaker pipe* has practically revolutionized horticultural endeavors ranging from ornamental gardening to cotton production. This inexpensive low-tech innovation also offers tremendous benefits for small-scale marijuana production. By delivering exactly the right amount of water directly to root areas, buriable soaker pipe can be used to maximize plant growth and flowering while creating a soil environment favorable to aeration and earthworms but discouraging to diseases and insect predators.

Unlike regular soaker pipe, which runs above ground, buriable soaker pipe can be installed beneath the soil surface. The outdoor or guerrilla cannabis cultivator may be particularly interested in the security advantages this invisibility can afford. Buriable soaker pipe also leaks evenly across long stretches under minimal water pressure. These characteristics allow the outdoor grower to select the most discrete locations on a property for individual plants or small groups and supply all of them with an ideal level of water, nutrients, warm air, and carbon dioxide through a single low-visibility system combining buried soaker pipe with ordinary pipe and hose. The plants can be located at different levels as long as the system is set up so that water flows from high to low.

The Cultivator's Handbook of Marijuana by Bill Drake describes in detail systems using buriable soaker pipe for a variety of indoor and outdoor growing situations. Drake's book is an excellent starting point for those interested in the nuts-and-bolts of buriable soaker pipe.

21. Polyploid Mutations

There have been experimental attempts to induce mutations in marijuana by means of X-rays and gamma radiation. These electromagnetic frequencies affect the genes and chromosomes and result in alterations in the plant's characteristics. Unfortunately, their work is chaotic and unpredictable and almost always produces useless distortions.

Colchicine

Far better results have been obtained by treating either the seeds or seedlings with colchicine, a toxic alkaloid derived from the autumn crocus (*Colchicum autumnale*). Normal plants (*diploids*) have two sets of chromosomes per cell. Colchicine treatment causes a dividing of the chromosomes, resulting in 3, 4, or 5 sets per cell. These plants are known respectively as *triploids*, *tetraploids*, and *pentaploids*.

Generically, any plant containing more than two sets per cell is known as a *polyploid*. These plants are larger, healthier, and more resistant to disease than normal diploids. They have darker and more abundant foliage. The flowers, pollen grains, and seeds are larger. The resin production is greater, and the isomeric rotation of THC is inclined to be higher.

Colchicine Toxicity

Colchicine is a very toxic substance. Those who work with it wear rubber gloves to prevent absorption through the skin and a breathing mask to prevent inhalation of the dust. Leaves that have been exposed to colchicine will be poisonous if smoked or consumed, although later foliage and flower tops, as well as plants grown from treated seeds, present no problem for marijuana consumers.

How Colchicine Is Used

There are several methods of treating plants with colchicine.

Dunking The Plant

When the plants are in the process of being transplanted, the entire plant including the roots is dunked in a solution of 1 gram of colchicine in 1 liter of water and planted. This method brings good results, but many of the plants will not survive the drastic treatment. Those that do will be polyploids.

Young polyploid leaf
Photo by Bob Harris reprinted from *Marijuana: The Cultivator's Handbook* by Bill Drake.

Soaking The Seeds

The seeds are soaked overnight in a solution of 100 mg of colchicine in 100 ml of distilled water (the same dilution as for plants, but less solution is needed) and planted in the normal manner. The seeds that survive treatment and germinate will be polyploids. This method is almost as effective as treating the live plants. Growers prefer it because they are more willing to sacrifice 60-80 percent of the seeds than the same percentage of 8 week old plants.

Dusting The Ova

The ova of the female plants are dusted with powdered colchicine before they are pollinated. The seeds produced are planted. These plants will be dwarfs. Upon maturity the males are allowed to pollinate the females, but the females are protected from pollination from any other male plants. The seeds produced by this mating are polyploidal and will develop into giant plants of great potency. As long as pollination from alien males never occurs, all of the seeds produced in future generations of these plants will also be polyploidal.

How Colchicine Is Obtained

Colchicine is difficult to obtain. Names of chemical companies which carry it are listed in the directory entitled *Chemical Sources USA*, which is found in the reference section of most university libraries.

22. Cloning

 Cloning, the practice of growing plants from cuttings taken from a selected Mother plant, is a great way to rapidly generate harvest after harvest of marijuana of consistent quality.

While clones are actually made from cuttings, the term "clone" refers to the fact that all plants so produced will have the same genetic material as the Mother plant. Clones grown in the same environment as the Mother plant will be identical to the Mother as well as to each other.

Clones of clones can be made, as can clones of clones of clones, and so on. At least theoretically, therefore, the desirable characteristics and high quality of the original Mother plant can be preserved and propagated indefinitely through cloning as long as the growing environment is kept consistent.

Advantages of Clones

The age of the clone is actually the same as that of its Mother plant. A clone taken from a six-month-old Mother and grown for a month is actually seven months old, and produces THC with the potency of a seven-month-old plant as opposed that of a one-month-old. Clones taken from sufficiently mature plants can be induced to flower as early as two weeks after they have been rooted. Thus, cloning can be used to cut in half the time required to produce a mature crop. Cloning is also convenient because cuttings taken from the same plant at the same time will, in the same environment, grow and mature at a uniform rate, making the crop easier to house and care for.

Disadvantage Of Cloning

The only disadvantage of cloning is that it preserves and propagates genetic weaknesses as well as genetic strengths. The genetic uniformity of a clone population may therefore present problems when sudden or unpredictable environmental stresses or traumas, such as pests and disease, come into play. The genetic differences found in a population grown from seed guarantee some degree of variance in individual capability to cope with such events, bolstering the chances that a portion of the crop will survive. All members of a clone population, however, will be affected pretty much the same way. If the clone is genetically ill-suited to survive the onslaught, then the entire crop may be lost.

Rooting Cuttings

A female at least a month or two old is used as the Mother plant in cloning. Cuttings are taken from tips of lower, older branches that are healthy and firm. A clean, 45-degree cut is made halfway between two of the nodes from which the leaf clusters extend. Two or three sets of leaves and buds are trimmed from the part of the stem that will be placed below the soil line, leaving one or two sets of leaves above. The cuttings are put immediately in fresh, tepid water in which they are left overnight without light.

Small containers or nursery flats are used for rooting the clones. Root cubes or peat pots are convenient when it comes time to transplant them. It is preferable that the cuttings are rooted in coarse, clean sand or an artificial rooting medium such as vermiculite or perlite, but sterile potting soil will suffice. Holes slightly bigger than the width of the stem are poked in the rooting medium with a pencil or other appropriate tool, leaving at least an inch and a half of rooting medium beneath the hole to give room for roots to grow.

Nutrients For Rooting

A commercial formula for stimulating root growth is applied to the cuttings, the cuttings are placed in the holes, and the rooting medium is gently packed around them. A first light watering, leaving the surface evenly moist, should be performed with a solution containing vitamin B_1.

Lighting For Rooting

Eighteen daily hours of fluorescent light is ideal for rooting cuttings. The clones require a high level of humidity, which can be maintained by placing them in a plastic tent or other structure that holds in moisture or by misting them several times daily. Temperature should be kept at 70-80 degrees F. The cuttings will develop root systems sufficient for transplanting within one to four weeks. Further details on this procedure for rooting cuttings can be found in Jorge Cervantes' *Indoor Marijuana Horticulture, Totally Revised*, which contains abundant information on the theory and practice of cloning. Another valuable source of practical knowledge on this subject is Robert Connell Clarke's *Marijuana Botany: The Propagation and Breeding of Distinctive Cannabis*, which also describes an alternative technique for making clones known as *layering*.

Transplanting Clones

Transplanting is very traumatic for plants. Root systems, especially the tiny root hairs, are sensitive and easily damaged. Being as gentle as possible while transplanting is therefore key. Transplanting is best performed towards the end of the day so that the plant can use the night as a recovery period. The period of time that the roots are out of contact with soil or rooting medium is kept to an absolute minimum. The cuttings are transplanted into the same kind of soil that they were rooted in, or, if a soilless rooting medium such as perlite or vermiculite has been used, as much of the medium as possible is shaken off, taking care not to hurt the roots, before the plants are placed in soil. If a root cube or peat pot has been used, it is just set right into the soil.

After transplanting, the clones are watered generously with water that has been treated with vitamin B_1 or a nutrient formula that contains it. For the first few days after transplanting, the clones are exposed only to gentle, subdued, or filtered light, as growth must not outpace nutrient and water absorption, photosynthesis, and other metabolic processes that slow down while the clone convalesces from the shock of transplanting and adjusts to its new root environment.

Conclusion

Marjuana Cultivation
For Medical Use

 The knowledge and techniques described in this book have accumulated from hundreds of years of marijuana cultivation around the world.

In recent decades, the collective storehouse of marijuana-growing wisdom and know-how has vastly expanded, significantly increasing the information and options available to the curious and committed cultivator. The surge of progress in this area, driven by advances in horticultural science and the growing demand for fine marijuana among connoisseurs and people using marijuana medically, can be credited to the perseverance and ingenuity of growers and researchers everywhere.

The renewal of interest in marijuana's important medical benefits provides impetus for continued acceleration in the art and science of cultivating marijuana. With the evolution of an alternative network for meeting medical marijuana needs and the beginnings of legal protection for personal medical cultivation, the individual and community medical garden comes to occupy an increasingly central role. All of these developments add an extra dimension of gravity to care and dedication in growing marijuana. The widespread dissemination of information in this area now carries the hope of easing intolerable suffering and prolonging human lives. Excellence and expertise in cultivating marijuana are now more important than ever before.

Bibliography

Abel, E. L., *Marihuana: The First Twelve Thousand Years*, Plenum, 1980.

Bennett, Chris, Lynn Osburn and Judy Osburn, *Green Gold The Tree of Life: Marijuana in Magic and Religion,* Access Unlimited, 1995.

Boire, Richard Glen, *Marijuana Law, 2nd Edition*, Ronin, 1996.

Burgess, G. Anthony, *Indoor Sinsemilla*, G. Anthony Burgess (self-published), 1984.

Carver, G. W., *How to Grow Marijuana Indoors for Medicinal Use*, Sun Magic Publishing, 1997.

Cervantes, Jorge, Robert Connell Clarke, and Ed Rosenthal, *Indoor Marijuana Horticulture*, Revised, (self-published) 1993.

Clarke, Robert Connell, *Marijuana Botany: The Propagation and Breeding of Distinctive Cannabis*, Ronin, 1981.

Conrad, Chris, *Hemp for Health: The Medicinal and Nutritional Uses of Cannabis Sativa* , Healing Arts Press, 1997.

Conrad, Chris, *Hemp: Lifeline to the Future*, Creative Xpressions, 1993.

Drake, Bill, *Marijuana: The Cultivator's Handbook*, Ronin, 1986.

Drake, William Daniel, Jr., *The International Cultivator's Handbook* Wingbow Press, 1974.

Flowers, Tom, *Marijuana Flower Forcing: Secrets of Designer Growing*, Flowers Publishing, 1997.

Gold, D., *Cannabis Alchemy*, Ronin Publishing, Inc., 1989.

Gottlieb, Adam, *The Art and Science of Cooking with Cannabis*, Ronin, 1993.

Grinspoon, Lester, M.D., and James B. Bakalar, *Marihuana: The Forbidden Medicine*, Yale University Press, 1993.

Herer, Jack, *The Emperor Wears No Clothes: The Authoritative Historical Record of the Cannabis Plant, Hemp Prohibition, and How Marijuana Can Still Save the World*, Hemp/Queen of Clubs Publishing, 1990.

Mathre, Mary Lynn, ed., *Cannabis in Medical Practice: A Legal, Historical, and Pharmacological Overview of the Therapeutic Uses of Marijuana*, McFarland and Company, 1997.

Mechoulam, Raphael, ed., *Cannabinoids as Therapeutic Agents*, CRC Press, 1986.

Mikuriya, Tod H., M. D., ed., *Marijuana: Medical Papers 1839-1972*, Medi-Comp Press, 1973.

Potter, Beverly A. and Dan Joy, *The Healing Magic of Cannabis*, Ronin., 1998.

Rathbun, Mary, and Dennis Peron, *Brownie Mary's Cookbook and Dennis Peron's Recipe for Social Change*, Trail of Smoke Publishing , 1996.

Robinson, Rowan, *The Great Book of Hemp: The Complete Guide to the Environmental, Commercial, and Medicinal Uses of the World's Most Extraordinary Plant*, Park Street Press, 1996.

Rosenthal, Ed, Dale Gieringer, and Tod Mikuriya, MD., *Marijuana Medical Handbook: A Guide to Therapeutic Use*, Quick American Archives, 1997.

Rosenthal, Ed, *Marijuana Growing Tips*, Quick American Trading, 1986.

Shulgin, Alexander T., Ph.D., *Controlled Substances: Chemical and Legal Guide to Federal Drug Laws*, Ronin, 1992.

Stafford, Peter, *Psychedelics Encyclopedia*, Third Expanded Edition, Ronin, 1992.

Starks, Michael, *Marijuana Chemistry: Genetics, Processing, and Potency*, Ronin, 1990.

Storm, Daniel, *Marijuana Hydroponics: High-Tech Water Culture*, Ronin, 1987.

Todd, Larry S., *Dr. Atomic's Marijuana Multiplier*, Ronin, 1998.

CPSIA information can be obtained
at www.ICGtesting.com
Printed in the USA
JSHW051324140921
18719JS00001B/1

9 780914 171942